THE SPELL

POETRY FOR THE MODERN WITCH

Cover Art Copyright © 2022 by Indie Earth Publishing x Tanya Antusenok
Illustrations Copyright © 2022 by Tanya Antusenok

Edited by Flor Ana Mireles

1st Edition | 01
Paperback ISBN: 978-1-7379393-6-8

First Published October 2022

For inquiries and bulk orders, please email:
indieearthpublishinghouse@gmail.com

Indie Earth Publishing Inc.
| Miami, FL |

INDIE EARTH
PUBLISHING

THE SPELL JAR

POETRY FOR THE MODERN WITCH

"TO ME, A WITCH IS A WOMAN THAT IS CAPABLE OF LETTING HER INTUITION TAKE HOLD OF HER ACTIONS, THAT COMMUNES WITH HER ENVIRONMENT, THAT ISN'T AFRAID OF FACING CHALLENGES."

- PAULO COELHO

ALCHEMY AND THE ORACLE

COMMUNICATING WITH COSMIC BEYONDS

𝔇IVINE 𝔇IVINATIONS

ALCHEMY AND THE ORACLE ·

You Say Witch Like It's A Bad Thing
Kimberly Kling

You say witch like it's a bad thing.

But,

I practice the magic of the cosmos—
of my own body,
supple and sensual
mountains of blessed terrain
and oceans of holy water
birthed from the womb of the Universe.

My sorcery is that of love—
a love that burns so deep for the world
it could light a million
fires under weary feet
and move them not to death,
but to action.

My potions are made for healing—
earthen roots reaching deep down
into the living belly of the Earth
resurrecting life
and stirring it into
the cauldron of our souls.

The crones and the Cailleach
the crows and cats,
dance in the shadows
casting wide webs of wisdom
from untamed women
who I belong to.

Those catatonic bodies preaching fear
who tried to kill the wild
of my bloodline
are no match
for the bursting heart
of divine truth.

My truth.

The one that withstood centuries
of misused power,
where we buried hope and resilience
deep within DNA
until it would resurrect
with swirling fury once again.

Now.
Us witches.
Called from the depths of the
Earth's untamed soul—
those insults are lost on us.

See, we know who we are.
We are here to rise from the ashes
whisper our wishes on the wind
stoke the fires of transformation
feel the tides of tumultuous waters
and grow our roots in that steady soil,
deep, deep down.

With the backing of eons of ancestors,
we will light the darkest days
with our wise, witchy magic.

Alchemists Wanted
Veronica Szymankiewicz

We are alchemists,
making love to our darkness
until it transforms into light,
shifting the whole damn paradigm
one soul at a time.
A new day is dawning
and the world will never be the same again.

The Goddess Is Home
Courtney Force

my body
sings the story
of reclamation

homecoming

the prodigal daughter
returns home
to her own body

awaken
the kundalini

revisit
every single story
wedged between
33 vertebrae

i dance
my body
electric

alive
with each
breath of life

the trauma
stored
in each tissue
dissolves
into gold

into the blessed lesson
it was always meant to be

my ancient soul
has always known
alchemy

but remember when i thought
i was too good for me
ashamed
of the reflection
i would see and
disappointed
in the manifestation of
someone
who seemed like
so much less
than the person
i thought i could be

now here i am
reclamation

traveling
along the threads of time
to remind
every past version of me
she has always been
whole-y

remember

as in
unite
all dismembered

parts of me

as in
return
as a member
of my body

my body
as my country
my first home
this is where i am from

no more vacancy
this is a full-time
lifelong occupancy

ring the bell
in the temple

the goddess is home

Möbius
Marissa Renee

Death is as inevitable,
as life is unstoppable.

A raven lays dead
by the roadside.

Dandelions sprouting
through the cement
of its unbeknownst grave.

Little fragile plants
who refuse to give up
on seeking sunlight.

Black feathers
blown away in the wind,
parted from its scattered remains.

Like a flame wisped into ashes.

Or the seed of a dandelion plucked by the breeze.

•••••••••

A deer skull lays nestled
beneath a fallen branch in the forest.

Fresh spring grass grows
through clean white bone.

Overturned, my eyes peer inward,
there is life still yet to be found.

A snail has made his home
in the stillness that death has left.

Cavernous cranium emptied
to create space for new embodiment.

An open cove where new beings
have found a place to grow.

••••••••

Last spring I made a grave

for the hermit thrush
who broke its neck
against the sliding glass door.

I laid her beneath the boxwood tree
on a bed of rose petals
and rhodochrosite.

This spring
the tree bloomed in full.

Her energy returned
and manifested in each new bud.

Like a kiss of life,
the full breath
of a silent song.

••••••••

In each moment

There exists
the eternal summoning
of life through the veil
of death.

The outpouring of a cup
as it flows
into the heart
of a new vessel.

Energy seeking to be reborn in each and every form.

Each drop of water a unique microcosm of the endless sea.

This is the romancing of
refracted energy.

Become. Return. Redirect. Enter Anew.

Part from what you have become;
        into the return.
Become into an aspect entirely new.

Like the sand in a timeglass,
        shifting balance
between one end and the other.

Or a wave in its perpetual motion.
Pushed onto the land,
and yet called,
in return to the sea.

A current on a journey with no final destination.

There is a satisfaction I find in that.

That all anything ever is,

and has been,

is energy in movement.

Like a möbius strip.
The line between life and death is thin.

Just when you've found the top you've reached the bottom,
and then you find the top again.

Ebbing
        Flowing.

Becoming.
        Unbecoming.

•••••••

One day I will experience my promised ending.
The life I know now will be gone,
but my energy will live on.

My mind will grow anew in the flowers and drift free in the
clouds.

I will see through the refreshing morning dew
which catches sunlight in a spiders web,
entranced like the many flies caught in its thread.

My heart will become the grass and the mountains and the trees.

My body and blood will become the soil,
and I will become the bones of the earth,
Like the animals and many ancestors
who sleep, crystalized, beneath my feet.

My dreams will cast themselves in starlight.

My wisdom will exist in the passing of time.

My spirit will live in the water and the wind.

And when it rains,
      and thunder crashes,

      you might hear me singing
            of a new life being born.

Creatures of Habit
Jacquelynne Faith

If you leave enough
everywhere feels like home
She could take to other planets
Like a goldfish to a bowl
Is she a creature of habit
If her habit is to change
If like frogs and butterflies
It's routine to rearrange

Comfort is relative
She makes mattresses of coves
So good at living on the edge
She could find corners on a globe
Cause she learned something from the moon
Her whole existence is a phase
Why not walk backwards 'round the world
If you'll land in the same place

As the work horses and mamas
As the herd, as the flock
With their structure, with their order
As if they can see the clock
When were you born
Where will you die
It's neither there nor here
In every role, in any language
It's all just Love and Fear

So she'll bring zombies back to life
Show her hometown outer space
She can't help that she's magic
So she'll try to save her race

She'll mark the dreamers with an X
So they know they're not alone
Because the treasure is the ones
With adventure in their bones
Others keep their ships in bottles
But they'll fight giants for their gold
Yet even Pirates get the message
When there's sand between their toes
Get high on flora and fauna
Hunt for other things that shine
You say you want nirvana
But you're just standing in line
So let's get our iridescence
From the rainbows and the pearls
Cause under papers and fluorescence
We're just hungry boys and girls

If you believe enough
Anywhere feels like home
But only the weak
Would ever try to keep
A mermaid in a bowl

Bracken

Jordan Nishkian

The patter of footfall:
brittle leaves crack beneath me, hard
ground spurts reverberations
through bone and marrow. Dust picks
up   with rushing soles until I
find the part that's mine, a clearing through screens
of bracken where brute sun smothers withered sod.
Each dry breeze risks igniting brush.

Smoothing away husks
and branches, I remove my shoes. Air sucks
through teeth as uncalloused flesh discovers
burrs and thistles, wanting for crimson.
Arches sink past heels, toes burrowing into
summer-baked soil, digging through
planes of drought and umber. Before
closing, my eyes flash with a tan blur

—a buck sloughing velvet.
I sync abyssal breaths to buzzing and birdsong.
With the splintering of each nerve, warm
skin contracts, tightening into hard, dark plates.
My toes delve deeper, furcating into
tunneling, dendritic networks, seeking
pockets of lost moisture. Rind climbs up
my legs, forming knots over bruises,

constellations of scars, bulging
where joints and vertebrae separate. Fingers reaching,
rhytidomes fuse and encapsulate my sapling
core, antennae and ungues explore
my barken body. Ribs collapsing,

15

swelling into concentric rings—
amber eyes open for the blackbird perched
on my shoulder: turned away, unafraid.

From tender places
of my arms, where skin is thin enough to route
blue courses of stretching vein, buds
rupture, petals unfurling to brace
the open. Heavy clouds roll over, hushed
chills lift hairs into stems of waxen leaves, mist
slicks and weighs on mossy locks. Looking up,
I welcome the patter of rainfall.

Karmic Connections
Alicia Ayala (Blue Mystic)

Why is it
that my soul only craves you?

Why is it
that when we're together
it feels like we are worlds apart?

Why am I haunted
by the thought of you?

It's almost as if
we must have fell in love
in the wrong dimension

Or worse—
in a lost world

Baño
Annie Vazquez

A woman knows how to heal herself by
Submerging in a tub of water, brimming with flowers.
Rose petals, Marigolds, Lavender,
The cure for tears, anger, and fear.
Every time she scrubs a soapy petal to her skin,
It peels off her one by one.
And you doubt magic exists?

SIGNS
Clair O'Connor

oh fire signs,
you are passion and boundless energy.
you are the first, the galvanizer and the forger of paths.
others follow your lead but do not let weight of responsibility
smother your flame.
oh water signs,
my dear, you do not need to dilute yourself.
let them drown if they cannot handle your emotional seas and
let the steady flow of knowledge and service guide your current of
energy. we need you, more than you realize.
oh air signs,
my relentless thinkers. you see so much. you know by doing and
you must keep going. do not let the many decisions to be made,
paralyze you from taking flight. the wind might change, but you
know what you can handle. go forth without fear.
oh earth signs,
you are allowed to love. you are allowed to be soft, you do not
always have to be the rock between them and the Hard Place. you
are allowed to have fun and be a joyous child. give up control, at
least for a little while.

Flight of the Raven
Jacob R. Moses

Young Raven watched the carnage from afar
For hospitality was null and void
What once was a Jewish sanctuary
Became a pit of doom in Latvia

She watched their population get slaughtered
She'd soar - led only by her keen third eye
Throughout the whole time-space continuum
Her journey was that of a kindred sage

Her feathers black, transmuted her world red
Gold fields surrounded where her feet had perched
Upon the coat of arms denoting Preiļi
Her heart hurt as she watched the bodies drop

She called upon her ancestors as guides
One century prior in Baltimore
Where one elder raven bestowed warning
Upon a poet mourning his soulmate

Young Raven processed all the pain retained
Accepted her role as a spectator
To see through injustice and false logic
Yet still be an eyewitness of true love

untitled
Lianne Quintero

She dances
She paints
She writes
She moves

Her limbs
Her bones
Her heart
Replied

"There is no room
In this vessel,
To store
Pain."

So, we move
Dance
Paint
Write

And create space
For the pain
To alchemize
And turn

To love

Magical Thinking
Veronica Szymankiewicz

I wish my crystal ball wasn't on the fritz
and my tarot cards would just stop having fits,
purposely omitting all the important bits.
Maybe, just maybe, I could foretell our future
together as well as a famous fortune teller.
Perhaps, I could channel the great Nostradamus,
politely asking him for prophecies
regarding the veracity of your promise.
I can always try to divine with the help
of some tea leaves,
wait for signs from the Universe, or even attempt
to interpret my convoluted dreams.
It's possible the stars and planets
could hold all the answers..
Maybe, I'll even get lucky with some guidance
from the Ascended Masters.
If only I had the power to read your thoughts
in order to comprehend your true intention.
Is any of this real or all just a cruel invention?

untitled
Victoria Clara

Holding hands with my sisters as we chant spells of love for her
not for them.

Taking from the earth only to give it right back, repurposing
her energy to bend it to our will.

Knowing that magic is white and black because Mother Nature
is both beautiful and cruel.

One can not exist without the other.

♋
Lindsay Valentin

I am a child of the midnight water
crab baby
moon warrior
born with waves in my aorta
feldspar veins and
seaspray vocal chords

I am the ocean's lunar child
the sea's crescent daughter
I'm made of regolith and brine
élan vital of iron and water

untitled
Clair O'Connor

we playfully go where we are not able to naturally.
the bottoms of the sea,
free falling through the air.
we make silly games out of sticks and stones and lines in the
sand.
we make our homes beautiful, like song birds weaving twine into
their nests—
after all, it is just somewhere to land.
we are all crawling towards an inevitable future, an eventual
heartbreak.
but we go forth with laughter, hands held together.
we pluck the strings of life and find our ancient chords, and tether.
we dance and drink and swear and smoke,
plant and harvest, make delicious food,
and hope.
we consume and consume.
and still we might feel empty.
but there is a lovely alchemy
where we get to decide,
what should the next adventure be,
and will you be by my side?

The Scars of the Soul // Akashic Records
Alicia Ayala (Blue Mystic)

I have a fascination with words
There's something ethereal
about verbal communication

It's perhaps the greatest gift
of the physical realm
For in the Universe
We speak only in energy

The infinity of language
is reminiscent of the vastness
of The Universe

There lie the mirrors of the soul
internal scars, pure intention
through words and feelings
and divine intervention

Words are messages
Words bring meaning
All transmitting to memories
From this life
To your immortal being

In the Universe
There are no words
Only the energy
Brought upon by
that infinite collection of memories

That's why it is so important
In this life

To not leave things unsaid
To only say what you mean
To be gentle with others
As you would be yourself

Use your words wisely
For they may cut too deep

And just like energy can never be destroyed
Your words may never be forgotten

COMMUNICATING WITH COSMIC BEYONDS

A RIPPLE IN THE VEIL
Madeleine S. Cargile

Does death hollow one to a rotten core?
Does all that's lovely melt to gore?
Plump lips shrivel; rose cheeks sink,
Bones grow brittle; broke teeth clink.
Can magic spark star-crested veins?
Bring back her life to full again?
Lighten dim eyes; twitch finger tips,
Filter wax guise; open blood drips,
Wisps of blackness conceal the sight.
What will it be when I spare my might?
Will I be greeted with a horrid fright?
Or will my beloved be all that's right?

I peel back the veil; pray pride not consume me.
A trill ices veins—oh could this a ruse be!
I take her hand, soft as silk,
I take in eyes, glassy milk.
My heart stutters, filtering night,
Hands rise to hold a face so bright.

When I kiss her, she smiles, and my fears flake to dust.

To Death and Back
Flor Ana

I'll sink myself into the soil, allowing
my limbs to become mycelium
and send nutrients to the trees.
I'll become their highway
of information and secrets
and maybe, just maybe,
I'll hear the truth about the skeletons in the closet, of
what happens after death, after an icy veil forms over our eyes
and our bodies metamorphosized, rigor mortis setting in.
Maybe, just maybe,
I'll learn the truth of where you've gone, of
where we will all go one day, the parade of balance,
a heaven and hell dichotomy that only seems to exist
on this materialistic, silently spiritualistic, plane.

If I get no answer from conversing with the seeds and the trees,
I'll dig deeper.
I'll sink myself further until my aching limbs
have reached the earth's core, and from there, I'll do more.
I'll do all I can to hear your voices again, see the way you shined.
I'll go to the measures of speaking to the divine,
of communicating with every single carcass
that had disintegrated into the roots of the earth,
already in another life, in another existence, in another realm.
I'll become death itself if that means I know what happens next,
what happens when we take our final breath.

Then, I'll come back, sliding my way out from the mantel,
lava burning me from the inside out.
I'll shake the decay off my calcium-deprived bones and
twist and twist and twist
until I reach the level of soil where I once was,

a new terrain now from how long it took me to return.
I'll beg the trees for my life back,
to send me the nutrients they
send each other, for I, too, am the forest's daughter
and just want to see another day of sunlight,
rays shining above my head, crowning,
making their way into my tangled, knotted hair.
I'd promise to brush it every morning in the mirror
if only they'd let me see
another day.

Eventually, with my crying pleas, they'd listen,
sending their nutrients through me,
to the mycelium that is my limbs, my heart,
until slowly, like a zombie,
I will return from
the grave, the underground, the underworld,
and I'll run straight towards my mother and father,
dirt and grime staining my cheeks,
soil beneath my fingernails, a smell
of decay, and earth and love emitting through the entire globe.
With tears running down my face, reaching down my filthy neck,
I'll tell them what I learned,
not just for them, but for myself.
I'll tell them with my hoarse, yet soothing, voice,
"They're okay where they are now,
and we will be, too, when we get there."

The Fae
Sofia Iriarte

Though my garden might be tempting,
for which a stone circle might appear,
must beware for the fae are calling,
Thus it's not a game, thus thou must fear.

They hide in thickets,
They hide in groves,
They hide in bouquets,
They hide in coves.

Thou must never cast a such spell,
for which they'll undoubtedly respond,
must beware for an offering, an eggshell,
Thus it's not a game, thus thou have a bond.

They take your name,
They take your infant,
They take your flame,
They take your significant.

Thou must be warned to not show grace,
Thou must be warned to not say thou name,
Thou must be warned to not cast this spell,
Thou must be warned to not taunt the Fae.

Thicker Than Water
Jordan Nishkian

With a twist, water
      beats on to acrylic,
   heating my familiar
         place behind fogged glass.
     Narrow streams comb
through and wet my hair,
   pulling the curls
        past my waist till my knees
         bend and rest against
     the shower floor—
trickling over skin
        shooting off fingers
      puddling in pockets of bone and flesh.

I think of Nabia cutting green earth
        with rivers, of Ràn in icy fjords collecting
      her drowned, of Astghik
    bathing in the Euphrates, of Tsovinar
calling down rain in her fury, of

   grandmothers wetting their hands
before kneading dough or
    throwing water behind me
      after kissing goodbye (one,
    two, three times), of

the ridges of my fingertip
   in the stoup, sopping up
     holy water—dripping
        heavy from my forehead,
  —sometimes enough
     to crash into my heartbeat.

The Stalwart Coven
Hayden Kasal-Barsky

The universe calls for those who are magical,
with hands touching those far in Scotland,
deep in the Norwegion forest
along the coast and through Rome's ancient cathedrals.
The universe calls for women with crooked noses, broken feet,
children still clenching the breast of their mother
and men with uncleaned linens and full grown beards.
The universe calls us to be quiet but humbly powerful,
to keep one eye on God and the other towards
the society that rejects magic.
Be seen, my magical friends,
And reach out to the dead for guidance
if you ever forget how to live.
Necromancy is valid, our magic is valid,
and our souls forever belong to our sisters and mothers.
The magic of the world never deterred them.

untitled
A. K. A

Sitting in a circle to protect
With eyes fixed on the moon
My pendulum swings
As a steady heart beats
Calling upon her light
I cast down the powers
She willingly gives from the divine
To be one with all energy
A celestial being in me and in you
Beckoning her mysticism
Work in a quick spell or two

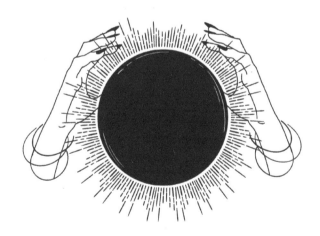

Necrophilia
Kendall Hope

I mustn't be attracted to what is dead inside you
Your mummified heart has left scratch marks on my mind

I am in love with the dead version of you
Craving the depths of an older soul
Staring into the eyes of a zombie in old photos
I cannot summon you into this new life

I mustn't make love with this corpse
But you Rest In Peace in my memories
from before death overtook you
You were never real and always a ghost
Now I must live with the chill of your cold blood

Two Spirits
Lindsay Valentin

late at night after the whole landscape has quieted
only the moon and I to witness the fire
the stars burning eternally
and smoke in my hair
after we bathed in sunflower petals and leaves of
exotic eucalyptus
after cleansing our spirits in sound in the vortex
asana and sun salutations between two joshua trees
micro/macro
the zoom out/the zoom in
remember universal love
let yourself feel it in your skin, in your bones, in your organs,
in your marrow, in your blood, in your cells, in your DNA
he speaks to you through water
she speaks to me through rainbows
held in the heart space
one hand to my breast and one on the belly
transmission coming from sunset
like the vibration of the sculpture we sat forth of
its magnificent hands bringing in the energy
of time immemorial
the crescent on its forehead the marking of the place
that I came from
the call of the feral
red blood buried under the joshua tree
behind a table of skulls and crystals
skeletons and revelations
make me a conduit, please use me
please make me a vessel for love
we are two spirits you and I
not 100% but 200%
I feel you, do you feel me?

The Scorpion, The Eagle, The Phoenix
Alexa Park

rising
from a lifetime of slumber,
dying
reborn
crawling through summer
forgetting
Finally,
the dream that froze the sky.

blinking Open
dusty eyelids,
finding somewhere
in the iris
a secret they left,
a secret they forgot
they left us,
hidden in plain sight.

they left us.

Here.
in the ash
of tomorrow,
where they thought they left us for dead.

in the trenches
with our eyes sewn shut,
like the hollow men,
mistaking the Nightmare
for the absence of Light.

but the moon is pulling the strings

Tonight.
the moon is pulling the thread,
and we begin to open our eyes.
the moon is illuminating
threads tonight
freeing
the frozen sky.

flooded with codes
written in stardust,
we read them proud and aloud.
we read them aloud
to our brothers and sisters
we see them
with our new eagle eyes.

What they say is,
Surrender.

this transformation is water.
this transmutation is fire.
the way leads to Pluto.
the change comes from Mars.

the day
is raining seeds that
spark an ember.
the rays
are catching weeds that
start a Fire
from which
we,
subjectively burn.

a pyre,

a funeral pyre,
from whom
we,
collectively breath.
first breath,
after a coma.
smoke free
only
footsteps,
heartbeat.
beginning again.

commanded now to
confront thy soul's contract,
although I've
signed it before.

a million times before,
and disobeyed myself
a million more.

although I've
transgressed the phoenix…
the mo(u)ring air
moves
fresh in my lungs.

You Are Everything
Veronica Szymankiewicz

Child, do you hear those rumblings deep within?
Perhaps, they are still indiscernible whispers in your heart.
You may not yet comprehend the ancient calls,
coaxing you to awaken and remember who you are.

You are powerful magic and ancient stardust.
You are the brightest light and the darkest of nights.
You are raging fire, oceans of the deepest blue, the winds that
speak forgotten knowledge to the trees, and the fertile Earth that
provides sustenance to all.
You are the beginning and the end.
You are dreams made flesh.
You are the Universe incarnate
with starlight dripping from your pores.
You are the grace of Heaven and the Nine Circles of Hell.
You are the rhythmic beats that seep into the soul, and move all
who hear into an all-consuming trance.
You are art that makes others weep.
You are endless love, breathtaking beauty,
the womb of all creation, and ruthless, unforgiving destruction.
You are One with all the people who have walked this Earth
since the dawn of time.
You are every language ever spoken
and every religion worshipped.
You are omniscient and immortal.
You are raw truth, pure sensuality,
and the delicious warmth of home.
You are both an ethereal angel and a sword wielding goddess
who makes the Devil himself bow down to your greatness
and quake in reverence.
You are the miracle of Life and Death
and all the unseen worlds in between.

You. Are. Everything.

Listen Child, the whispers have become urgent and clear,
yelling, tugging relentlessly at your heart.
It is time to wake up…
It is time to accept the power you have hidden deep within.
IT IS TIME TO RISE AND REMEMBER WHO YOU ARE!
It is time to finally see yourself reborn into your true form
once again…
A sword at your hip, faithful dragon at your side,
fire burning in your eyes, all knowing smile— equal parts
seduction and devastation on your lips,
and shining so damn bright you are the lighthouse that guides
all lost souls home.

Remember and accept you are divine and whole,
you always were.

In the Dark Woods Humming
Victoria Lynn Beckett

I am building a house for us
as I weave our roots
and stack the boards
that will keep out our old monsters

Your hand possesses mine
through each nail and leaf
my fingers place
Your shadow building with me
piece upon piece

I'll make the curtains
tendrils of my hair

I'll make the lamps
moonlight in Your eyes

I'll make my hearth
Your beating heart

I'll make the night wind creaks
the knocks of our feet when we dance

so when Your weary seeking
meets mine at our doorstep

you'll know you've come home.

Back
Elyse Rintelman (voidbird)

She is returning
Holon over holon
Wholeness over wholeness
To her waking self
To the body she forgot

She re-limits herself to form
In the beauty of decay I find her
Folded gently into the spaces
Between rot and sugar

Aromatherapy
John Queor

There are fresh lavender flowers
Rubbed in the ends of my hair
So the scent is carried in the wind
To travel up your nose alone
Causing you to investigate
To find the root of the scent
To find yourself amongst me
Lying on the long grass
With your head in my lap
Collecting wild violets
You'll exhale long and hard
As you talk about your travels
The trials and tribulations
All the time it took you
To find me right here
And now
For the very first time
In your whole life
You can talk
And someone will listen
Digesting each syllable
Basking in the breeze
Florals meandering
Falling on your skin
Relaxing your frown lines
I cradle you and listen
Even after the sun sleeps

Burning Man
Jacob R. Moses

Black Rock City—a desert filled with haze
Their rings had glistened as their fingers tanned
Upon the playa, Moonchild caught the rays
As Krishna lay beside her in the sand
Eloping without blessings from their folks
Their honeymoon was marred by dissonance
But Krishna's optimism was a cloak
And Moonchild's tears were dried by his sixth sense
At Burning Man, stars would illuminate
Community under Orion's belt
They wished they didn't have to ruminate
But insecurities would surely melt
The newlyweds had watched the wood man burn
Disapproval: no longer a concern

May
Maverick L. Malone

prophecies whispered
from this once pale earth
now dotted with the patina of settled wisdom
in thulian pink and mulberry
thriving below the rich fern canopy
where my high cotton congruence
hangs like fresh laundry on the line

I let my bare body ask for what it wants
and then listen closely:

sink into me
rest and read
filling the sacred sacral
fodder for the feast of creative prowess
light magic to be absorbed
explored
embodied
embraced

breathe
ground
make space

the witch's homecoming awaits

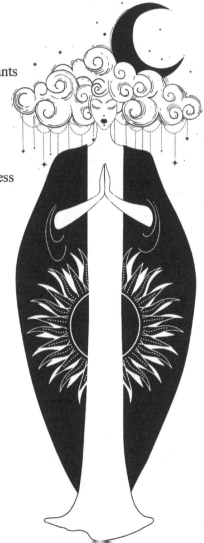

She, an inside out rainbow
Amelie Honeysuckle

A moment of hello
She, a flame of violet
Smiles in bubbles
Pop, Pop, Pop

A moment of experiences
She, a smoke of roses
Colorful in her energy
She rises
Touching my aura

A moment of transformation
Mostly for me
She, a moment of serenity
The mountains melt
The trees dance for me
Love infuses my entire being

A moment of rainbow
She, an eternal being I had to of once known
We converse
She has gifted me
And I have a new existence to love

She, a new passion
A luck of the draw
The one I knew I was meant to meet
Goodbyes made under the godfather tree
Leaves drop in spins
As my summonings walk away
With a skip in her step

Incantations and Elixirs

Ritual
Kira Rosemarie

My fingers go numb
holding an icicle as a wand,
cleansing the space of myself

and throwing black salt from the fire
over my left shoulder.
How much of ancient paganry

is a myth of our own making?
Each Yule I think of ancestry,
but they whipped

blood from tree branches
and I spill salt in a circle
guiding simple meditations

in a community of one,
the most ethereal connection
remaining behind wires and screens.

Rip linen through this dimension
and tie your eyes before history's shine,
forget what you've learned

of the past.
Carry forth blindfolded
into the future.

The Proper Use of Honey
Jordan Nishkian

In younger days, my mother taught me
  about the proper use of honey.
From the time clumsy fingers
   could lift my eyes above the kitchen counter,
    I remember the line of golden jars
   (each wrapped in its own colored ribbon),
sun shining through them like stained glass.

Of the five,
  I knew four well.

Every Sunday afternoon, she called me
  to the counter, with a teaspoon
    of the green jar and lifted it to my lips.
My tongue would stick to the roof
  of my mouth until it was loosened
by the cold glass of milk she tucked into my hand.
When warm winds rolled
  through Santa Ana, kicking up dust
    and cracking my throat,
  she tipped the purple jar until gold rippled into
a hot mug of chamomile—
and after my hair transmuted
  from straight lines to unpredictable curls,
   she dipped her hand into the yellow
  and mixed it with olive oil, calming each
coil above my neck and behind my ears.
She used the blue when I was wounded,
  to seal cuts and silence scars—
the night of one Fourth of July was spent
  covering my hand,
    speckled by blisters from a sparkler,

with honey bandages—
leaving a faint cluster I only see in certain light.

The jar wrapped in red
      evaded twenty years of questions.

On my first day of heartbreak, eyes swollen, head heavy,
      she greeted me at the counter with a rose
           she was growing outside the window,
      and twisted open the lid
through the crunching of crystals.
I watched her paint each point,
      sweetening the edges with her finger.
          "It's time that you know,"
      she said as she passed me the stem,
"the best parts of life
      are licking honey off a thorn."

Pick Your Poison
Kendall Hope

Pick your poison, they say,
so I stare at my potions and contemplate.

A deep burgundy stares me in the eyes.
Is this love that I'm needing?
No, I'm already tied to it.

How about this sickened chartreuse,
Will it take away my worries?
No, everything now is meant to exist.

The turquoise shimmers and glints,
to look makes me wince.
It creates more sorrows for one that borrows
the sadness from my heart to theirs.

So what poison do I pick?
Oh, I see, it must be to live with no magical solution.
To love and to heal and stick to what is real.

Lux
Laura Beth Johnson

I went off lithium.
"Typical for a bipolar," said the psychologist.

When my blood cleaned itself,
I woke up to my life.

My Body missed me.
        She met me in last night's sex magic ritual.

She said that the origin of energy is delight.
                She took me to Creation.

I saw the Intention of Being,
        folding and expanding within Herself—light.

Body showed me where she and I dwelled,
           twisted in the terrific kinetic tear.

She said we belong to each other.
        All of us, but especially she and I (a phosphorescence).

I was given an incantation.
           "Repeat and reveal," she instructed.

 I obey,   god that is my body, god that is my
liver, god that is my iris, god that is my skin, god that is my clit—

god in my body. god of my body. god, my body,
                                        I say, I say

I haven't worshipped like this since I was unmedicated.
mirages of myself in trees. thought I must be Christ hanging.

self-perception taken as easy as air.
I saw the canary dead and kept digging.

           Body remembers life's conception!
She felt it with her own time.

I process the dissonance:
           Illness cripples creatures as old as Health.

When there is not enough iron in my blood,
She makes me rock hungry.

When I need heat, she weaves air and hair.
We shivered before the invention of friction!

My space sharer, my teacher,
           They prescribed a flattener to keep me safe in Her.

           This vision is different. This altar has no sacrifice.
There is nothing to beg for, nothing to become.

           god in my body. god of my body. god, my body,
I repeat. I reveal. I understand She is holy. I understand I am holy.

I am on a new medication that tingles our feet,
but the doctor said that should go away.

I wish I could stay off sedatives, but I want Her
We both know I was right about Christ.

This pill and water,
                              Our bread and cup.

we long to unfold, to unite,
                              to create our own spark of light—

Bath Potions
Chelsea Miner

Scum-skinned bar soap is not
sacred on its own, but neither am I.
So when I, age six, peeled back
tender layers of lather with my thumb
and let them fall into the bath around me,
we both became holy to ourselves.

"A potion," I called it when Mom asked where
Dad's Barbasol had gone.
And it was.
Not waste, never
waste.
It was Passage;
first footfall into trusting that I knew
better than anyone what should be important
to me.

My bath potions were quiet
and important
and, yes, sacred—
a way I never felt
when the dusty reverend scolded me
and all of us for being
what we were: not holy
on our own.

One summer sundown some years after
my first potions, I leaned on the rotted fence
by my parents' barn and told the horse
I didn't believe in
God.
And everything replied

with enormous quiet.

I swirl that moment into my potions,
which are not sacred
on their own.

But neither am I.

Magic Words
Jacquelynne Faith

They don't call it "spelling" for nothing.

There is a "chant" in "enchantment."

Arts lost to time—and this is tragic.

Imagine what you'd bring to life…

If you only knew your words were magic.

GROW
Clair O'Connor

like things that grow
they strive and reach
for warm sun and peace at least
but sure enough they will find
some branches
are better off left behind
but sure enough that suffering plant
will grow twofold where one was last

Love Spells Love
Annie Vazquez

How to call in love:

1:
Set a fresh baked apple pie
doused with cinnamon, an
aphrodisiac that enchants with
loving whispers on your windowsill.
Let the aroma extend out like hands
reaching out into the air and plucking
your true love into your arms.

2:
Write them a love letter
Place it in a maraschino cherry-tinted envelope
Pour a teaspoon of sugar to
summon a sweet partner.
Add 5 crimson-tinted rose petals for
a love that continuously blossoms from
seed to rose each season.
Sprinkle a dash of sea salt to cultivate a pure love
that knows how to detox and always finds a way to flow.
Layer on lipstick the color of flames and
seal it with a loud kiss.
Muahhhhh.
Bury it inside an Anthurium plant
shiny like embers to
ignite a fiery passionate union.
The Greeks called them arrows of Cupid for a reason.

3:
Buy a pair of lace underwear and bra in bubblegum pink.
Stand in front of your mirror with your new set on.

Say: I love you. I am good enough. I am beautiful enough.
I am worthy enough and love begins with me.
I am a mirror of my relationships and I chose to reflect
the best in me now.

dinner with circe
Amalia Maria

she's not your usual long-haired, pointy-nosed witch
but a regular-looking girl, with a baby in her belly and a journal
full of oracles. she greets the men who come to her shore,
feels their eyes scan her body, and she knows they're hungry
for more.

like kings, they drink her red wine,
talk loudly over bread and butter,
undress her with their eyes. they don't know that she,
this pregnant beauty, she can see.
what's in their minds, she can read.

the loudest man stands, starts to make a scene,
his wine glass empty.
he grabs her from behind, pressing hard against curves,
he's ready. with
eyes closed, she's silent, taking every inch of meat. he feels
a sweet release, then his ears start to bleed. while he was inside
she cast a spell, using only her body.

down he falls, and his men's mouths open,
their chewing jaws drop.
none of them would live to tell of the pregnant witch
who let them in,
then sent them all to burn in hell.

Spellbound
Kendall Hope

I put a spell on you
with the flick of my hips.
In the dark with candlelight,
you are sewn to my lips.

My form is casted to your gaze
as the magic of your fingers trace my body.
My shadow dances among the walls
and your mind goes foggy.

I put a spell on you
with the entrancement of my being,
except this spell is not only from my power.
I have made myself to you, worth seeing.

May I be fertile in my essence and my practice
for a spell of love is rather romantic.
May this spell last and forever cast us,
for this love has no death.
Just pure magic that enchants us.

Craft
John Queor

When you bought me roses
I saved the thorns in a jar
In a mixture of cayenne
Black pepper and black salt

Kept secure in a cabinet
Shrouded in darkness
Pushed way in the back
Taut in a cool, dry corner

The moon is my crown jewel
The sun reveals the truth
The universe can be a tool
First utilized in my youth

I saw you in my mirror
Shooing off the crows
Your aura was so muted
To the freezer you must go

directions for (PROTECTION)
Heidi Valkenburg

1) wrap me in the weighted night
thick dark and whole
2) summon the silence of this cove; trace a wide circle in white
chalk—slowly—
3) don't you so much as whisper—or they'll hear
4) stitch up the sides of these edges
frayed precarious seams
leave me just a little room to breathe
5) lay fresh lavender and delicately drip orange oil by my crown
— place a small bundle of fresh
honeycomb nearby, should I need it
 6) scamper swiftly gather—burn a small lasting fire
7) finally—call the grey bird
deep holy below
and before you kiss my forehead in parting
—together sing me to sleep
ensure i hum a little; then you'll know it's time
leave me here, gently, like this—and I'll last a while
like this
i will last a while

A Spell Jar Recipe
Chelsea Miner

A jar-held coupling:
pregnant smoke and fertile air, ribboning
their shared hollow.
They make room for promise.

Next, from gentle hands, a little
bed of salt. Tides of
lavender from a tiny plastic bag—I have no
garden.

I sow it in with more
store-bought siblings and
water the strange strata, McCormick
herbs of Scarborough Fair,
with a drowning of honey.

Cork with pink wax and,
last, give it the company of
grace; know that no jar and no
herbs and no smoke can
add up into little ways you

love yourself
without your hand in the jar.

There's a Spell for That
Angelica Medlin

Magic is hard.

'Cause I thought it was the warm feeling
of putting on my costume every year,
waiting for the click of my dad's camera
as my mom pinched my ears.

Here it comes.

"It's demonic," she'd remind me,
"We only do this for fun.
God doesn't like these monster faces
That'll vanish with the sun."

"Why not?" I'd ask.

"You grew me with communion wine,
told me every Easter, Jesus is risen!"
"God works in mysterious ways," she'd say,
"And hell is a possible prison."

"But I'm good."

"The darkness comes in lots of different forms,
and the devil waits for our mistakes.
Keep praying," she'd say,
"Believing is all it takes."

"In what?"

"Come sit next to me in church this Sunday,
watch the white dove on its perch."

But she didn't pay attention
When I lost my faith in church.

"It's not bad."

Mixing lavender and chamomile aids sleep,
And messaging the temples brings calm.
I turned to science and need of proof
as my only soothing balm.

"This feels right."

I'll light a black candle to protect our home.
"Don't bring that dark into our house."
But we lit candles when grandpa passed,
and she was silent as a mouse.

I believe.

Burning incense helps me meditate,
and I bring my mom found gifts.
"What is this?" she asks, *"How does it work?"*
My answers have begun to heal our rift.

"Ah, está bien."

Now she sees the blackened candles,
politely turns her nose up, no fits to pitch.
But I don't think she'll ever like
that I call myself a witch.

A Spell for Healing
Trudy Hodnefield

I bury the dream where you are cutting into my thighs with your nails,

where I am pulling a rope that I cannot see the end of but keep pulling anyway.

I bury the exes

and the relationships that never had titles,

who I never had language for and so tripped, tongue over hand, into the next one,

and the next one.

I bury who I was when I mislabeled my own trauma.

When I thought pretending to stay asleep was the same as giving consent.

When I believed my heart was so heavy it deserved to sink my body with it.

I bury the way I treated people before I realized I was no longer defending myself, just clawing at those who were trying to understand.

I plant my apologies and water them with the way I move through the world now,

water them with my tomorrows,

fertilize the ground with the mistakes I will make in the future.

I do not believe buried things stay buried.

I know they come up again with the rain, and the floods, the excavations from the next time we try to build something here.

They come up through the roots of anything new that grows,

seep into the water of the nearest stream.

They become the rain clouds.

They become the rain.

I dig the ground a cavity.

Fill it with eggshells, and fingernails, and bad dreams.
Next to them, I place a photograph of my grandparents cutting the
cake at their wedding,
a photo of the tree tunnel on Kaua'i, the trees in the picture as still
as my breath while
my mom drove us through it.
I fill the mud of this place lovingly with old sorrows—
not gone-things, but old feelings that are always present,
quiet under the floorboards of each morning.
The dust that settles is swept away and always returns.
I dig and I bury,
I pat the earth back over itself with soft hands and wait to see
what new life brings.

Spells to Keep my Children Safe
Johanna Hatch

Take your child out beneath the full moon
In the cool night air, let her breathe
Whisper to the sky your supplication—

May this aching croup still
May she sleep

Hide hematite in his backpack
When the news tells you another school became
A cemetery today

Hold it to your whispering lips
And beg: not him, not mine

Gather strawberry stems, banana peels, sandwich crusts
Stir counter clockwise into the grass clippings
As the worms and spiders scatter

Chant three times:
May there be a future for us all

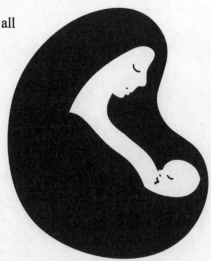

GROUND YOURSELF IN THE SOUL SOIL SMOKE

Can You Hear the Universe?
Tori Louise

Can you hear the universe?
It whispers to me
Inaudibly
Yet tangibly
Her breath caresses my soul
Like the breeze that flows through the canopies of trees

I feel my heartbeat in the soil
Deeper even
Past the bedrock
And the ancient lakes
In the core
It pulses and thrums
My blood and bones dance to the beat
Soon the knees of civilization will buckle under the heat
Of eons

Can you feel
The vibrations of space and time?
They run through my body
They rattle my bones with their song

Sometimes my body is so filled with the sound of movement
I surely must burst

Explode
Into a billion tiny molecules
Continue my ancient destiny
Our collective one

Expand
Grow

Create

What could it be searching for if this is all there is?

Grind
Javon Rustin

for those who hustle
& heave
& breathe heavy
hoping to afford more peace

who know how expensive
an easy breath can be
one free of stress & worry
of task & toil:

yes we on our grind
but won't be ground to dust. will
be grounded instead

our well-being well balanced
our work ethic rewarded in rest

Spirit Walking
Marissa Renee

Walking over Nisenan
And Wašišiw shadows

Their ancestry dancing
In the tips of the evergreens
And likenesses

Appearing in the faces
Of the mountainside

Souls that became Devas
To the ancient woods…

The Altar begins to set itself
A stone coyote skull at its center

Many crystals we present
And many we gather at our feet

Offerings decorated by mosses
And branches of pine

Balanced and equal placements
Attuned to the polarity of all things

The flame is struck
And incense qicks
In folds and spirals

We three
Sestras
Dance

And howl
And pour offerings onto the earth

Singing in silken smoke
And drinking from pink champagne
Blushing the color of the sky
Whose clouded wings
Expand in entrancing orange

We sit
And fill our three cups
While the last remaining light
Departs us

Watching
As sun sets

My eyes adjust
To the pitch of night

And in the airy darkness
I walk among spirits

Of the land and sky

Timeless and formless

Energies of the stones
And trees
And hollows

Their faces and bodies
Ether
Formed against the darkness

Water and the flow
Of the Aurora Borealis

Quintessential beings
Of eternal essence

A salamander made of starlight
Whose barium flame burns chartreuse
Amid an oceanic black skyline

A mountain cat cut from a nebula
Of fuschia and ruby
Glows her sly grin

Friendly guides
Who act as lights

Mimicking quasars
And astral bodies

They whisper to me
Their love for the forest

The land is their mother

As it is mine

I sleep safely

Atop the cliff
Beneath the stars

And awake
To the clarity

Of a pale blue sky

Brilliant sunlight refracts
Against chalcedony
And quartz monuments
And sparkles
In the dust beneath my feet

I think about our footprints
My sisters and mine
And those
Which once stewarded this landscape

And I think of the time before us all

Acknowledgments to Nisenan & Wašišiw land—the El Dorado National Forest.

Turn the Wheel
Allison Baldwin

1.

Remember the child that played in the dirt.
Remember the child that dirtied the dress.
Remember the kaleidoscope clouds—
The original storytellers—patiently waiting.

Remember the sun and its friendliness.
Remember the invitation to play.
Remember the generous earth.
Remember the way she covers you.

Remember your fingers are hers.
Remember your hands can hold her.
Remember this exchange of breath.
Remember this eternal life.

Remember to move with the wind.
Remember it watches your back.
Remember it gently carries.
Remember such keepers of ordered steps.

2.

Remember such keepers of ordered steps.
Remember the element of fire.

Remember the way we gather around
Ready to turn an ear.

Remember the voices that come to her side
Each to each so dear.

Remember the shadows her heat creates,
The outlines of ancestral desire.

Remember that each ordered step
Starts with a spark of fire.

3.

Remember such keepers of ordered steps.
Remember the element of air.

Remember to breathe deep
Giving thanks in morning prayer.

Remember each breath as an offering of love
To begin each day anew

Continue to rise above
Beyond past and present you.

4.

Remember such keepers of ordered steps.
Remember the element of earth.

Remember the soil
That created space well before your birth.

Remember the animals who listened for you.
Your distinct mating cry.

Remember it is your unlikely neighbors
Who will teach you how to

Fly.
    Fly.
        Fly.

5.

Remember such keepers of ordered steps.
Remember the element of water.

Remember to remain in flow
For you're an earthly daughter.

Remember an open heart
Keeps the waters clean

Consider dry spells opportunities
To remember the origins of your dream.

6.

Remember the child that played in the dirt.
Remember the kaleidoscope stories.
Remember the generous earth.
Remember you reflect all her glories.

Remember the generous heart that beats under your skin.
Remember the curious fingers that dig and dig and dig

Remember the soft mouth that speaks with deep conviction.
Remember to honor your steadfast intuition.

Remember to be patient with each elegant turn
Remember to always embody and learn.

Remember these ordered steps

For they are all we have
When we have lived the fullest life
And now we must turn back.

Turn the Wheel was inspired by two oracle cards, Turn and Remember, found in the Prairie Majesty Oracle deck created by Kara Simmons, with artwork by Amy Putney Koenig. The questions on the oracle cards are "What eternal knowledge can I access in human form?" and "What is next in my becoming?"

She is a Tree of Mossy Green
Amelie Honeysuckle

What once was
To what can be
Through focus and belief

What once was
To what actually is
By feeling the roots sprout
Out of your toes
And into the ground below

You are a vibrant green
Vines wrap around you
They bring you comfort
You are an old tree
And have learned from your years

What once was
To what is in front of you
Open your eyes
Slow your breaths
Sit in realization

Life in its beauty
Birds chirping
The silent hum of the room
The love others choose to show you

What once was
To what no longer exists
For you are here in the now
Your mindfulness sprouting below you
Accept where you are

And how far you have come

Your roots are deep in the dirt
You are powerful
You control your world
You make your own happiness
Because

What once was
No longer exists
You are here in the now
A beautiful old mossy green tree
Laced in vines
What once was
No longer exists

Vapors Curl and Dance
Flor Ana

Streams of smoke sit on the windowsill
Where the incense scents and falling ashes never sit still
They tickle the tangled strands of my hair
And you may read into what it means, but beware

There are so many silently spoken words within the smoke
That wrap around You and I like a lightly-fitted silver cloak
And the smells, the mists they bring with it are so divine
When read in certain ways, it may help you to align

To discover what the Universe has not written in the clear
To uncover what storylines and events may lie near
Listen to the strands of smoke that flutter about the air
Watch as the vapors curl and dance as they pay us cosmic fare

The messages may lie in the haze that they leave
And each dainty strand gives you reason to believe—
To believe in something bigger, more than just You and I
Providing more than reason to just simply feel Alive

Porch Swing
Jacob R. Moses

Stabilizing weight
resting laurels

upon polished planks
Underneath the moon

Sitting and rocking
At ease, carrying

mass by way of
sturdy cables

Suspended at this
moment, floating

Neglecting eventual touch
of feet against pavement

My Haunted House
Christian Colado

Dig a hole the magician did,
as the damned walk past his sweet trees.
Past the beautifully knotted wood,
they knock with tender ease.
Sunbeams land on the magician's eyes,
igniting pools of comfort.
Brown,
accepting eyes that search for your black-seeded sins
Near orgasmic came relief:
Lovingly plucking dark sins you ate
He invites you to gaze.

Soothing blue walls,
haunted by eternal comfort, his compassion.
Paintings lined his home.
Obscured from evil eyes, moments of passion.
Each claimed different aches,
his humming being the only remedy.
"Sooner or later,
griefs and woes become as painless as bittersweet melodies."
As we walked, the house diverged.
A labyrinth ranging human grace and disgrace.
More than just a haunted place.

Paintings turn to music, music into whispers,
whispers into pages
Pages into bedrooms;
secrets thrusted on him, sins become spaces
Miles into this haunted house,
the magicians conjured Eden's garden
Sprawling, spanning acres and acres.
On this magical plot of land

Black moons caressed sacred skies,
cleaning the fear and shame seeped within
"Sacred ground for planting sins."

"Planting sins is an art. To take the impure,
silence its cries, subdued."
As he watered it, colors cycled through the moon ending in blue
Clasp of hands, his eyes reflect the ghostly crescent,
the soil becomes aggrieved
Tales of devils, evils done,
become tree of breathe and bone freed
Branches scrape the skies, unfurling leaves and pollen,
scattering into starscapes
Thunderous sorrow flowed in his place

Apple shaped stars grew from bone white branches.
The magician smiled
"People's sins are not so bad,
they point to pains that poison inside."
He picks the fruit-shapes star
and tastes its white divine relentless ley lines
Juices nestled themselves in his beard,
my shames were crowned above him
Scanning them, one by one,
fear of judgment battered by every heartbeat
Till his presence stopped the shame

Language never herd before did outpour, soothing every secret
Ripping every sin kept hidden, giving me relief I've longed for
Then this saintly man,
perfumed with boundless love and understanding
Guided me before the tree and clenched my hands upon it.
Curling fingers 'round the fruit that bursted
forth from sins so bizarre
"Taste just how sweet you really are."

Ablution (A Ritual Bath)
Mia Mourn

My Baptist waits so patiently
Eager for my undress
To relinquish me of my day
Melt me with each caress

Romanced by wine and candlelight
I succumb to the heat
Tantalizing each inch of skin
I revel in defeat

So pleased to become one with me
And wash my sins away
Anoints me with a love potion
Seducing me to lay

Arousing my carnality
Where all constraints are slain
My Baptist waits so patiently
To worship me again.

Searching Smokestacks
Rachel Finkle

Incense lit
and wait.
Close your eyes
the spirits don't want you to see them as they arrive
wrapped in their robes
of blue, lilac, pale green
all tinged gray.

Open.
Look at the thread curling to the window—
shut that now.
Thank you.
Now see how it curves left, towards peace?
Hold out your hands
let the vapors wash the blood from your knuckles.

The spirits shape the smoke,
I only tell you what I see.
The tree you sat under as a child
is growing fruit. Not ripe yet, but give it a few years and
it will rain plums upon your shoulders.
Don't look so surprised
at how I knew the fruit—
your mouth is still stained
purple at the corners.

Your mother sends her love in waves
See the pattern, rippling up the stream?
The cherry is deepening
she wants you to know
that she is proud of you
and waiting.

She says,
Keep your shoes tied.
Don't cry, I have seen how her big hands fit over yours
and how it felt.
She is whispering your name in the haze
What would you like to say? I will let her know.

Of Flesh & Earth
Maverick L. Malone

palo santo intentions set
windows thrown open
the infusion of music, poetry and dance
into every sonorous word spoken
an invitation for love and magic
to fill every corner of the room
energy renewed as easily
as a changing of the guard
the highest order
protecting the most sacred
a sanctified home
a safe space
as am I
a mere vessel of the same

To the woman, the human, and the witch
Tess Rio

If you need to lay that mask down,
lay it down safely into the hands of the women that came
before you,
let the comfort of knowing that
they too were sensitive and powerful
fill your heart with warmth.

If you spill your blood,
remember the generations of survivors that are your ancestors,
let it strengthen you and inspire you
until you're replenished.

Remember that the spirits of the past
and your soul are one continuous entity connected by DNA.

You are never alone.

The Untaming
Jacquelynne Faith

I was half naked in the woods when I met her
And it was me but backwards
Untamed by reason, untainted by time
She knew only rhythm, spoke only rhyme

As if I'd squeezed myself back up through the hourglass
A slave freed by the wilderness
Emerged as the sand fell from my bones
And crawled and clawed my way back home
We converged at the river
Where the reflection was clear
It was I that was lost—
And she always here

I saw her tangled hair and called it a nest
Saw her nakedness and thought it best
Found that witches and wolves were the same in their breast

And I honored
The wild woman in me

Of Breadth and Leaves
Athena Edwards

My branches tend to reach out too far.
Brushing against walls. Against thorns.
Sometimes even forgetting
branches are supposed to grow leaves too.

So much focus on reaching. Connecting.
Not enough focus on growing. Living.

And so, when I am stretched so thin,
My color exchanged for sheer breadth,
My state neglected
in favor of the services I provide,

I remind myself
To send that energy
To my roots instead.

Ready as always,
My environment surges up to greet me
From the background
where, in my mind, I had accidentally pushed it.

The scent from a nearby candle
reminding me it's important to breathe.
The dirt between my toes
coaxing me into a deep stretch.
The ocean waves partner up too,
massaging out my long-worn muscles.
The breeze greeting my return
with gentle kisses upon my skin.

I can help everyone else later.

I'll topple over if I'm not connected to the ground.
For now, this moment is for me.
And maybe this time, I'll see some flowers.

Rebound
Andy Daniel Diaz (addingpassion)

Pulsating rays,
Energy waves.
They lift me up and show me the way.

Healing the pain,
Falling like rain.
The power within me cannot be drained.

Riding the high,
It's past midnight.
But I'm still on fire, maybe I should breathe deep and sigh.

Into the ground,
An energy rebound.
I channel it and slowly my spirit is unwound.

Tranquility and peace,
Tension released.
Until the next time the energy in me is unleashed.

Smoke and Retribution
Darya Rose

The prophets of the past rode camels to
deliver their deciphered messages from source.

I can't help but compare myself to the greats as I place
a camel blue between my lips.
With each puff, I ask God for guidance.
If the smoke trails to the left,
I know I need to recenter in my divine femininity;
if it plooms upward, the time to rise to the challenge is near;
if it scatters to the right, the chances of a new lover are high.

On my very best days, I swallow all of the smoke,
allowing no divine messages through.
A return to the abyss.

DIVINE DIVINATIONS

The Vortex, I: You
Lindsay Valentin

Joshua Tree vortex
fall in
like sound carries in rock formations
so close/far
cicadas, smoke, sand
elements primal in their petroglyphs
I build fire
bathe in Florida water
sit under the moonlight at midnight
recording its poetry
while the sun is sleeping
and I am creating a constellation of words
to explain the universe of you
love sacred like stones
its essence minerals and fauna in the water
my hand to my heart so deeply
and I look into my mirror
and you are reflected
the stars say ask
the fire says ask
your life is yours for this to decide
do you open yourself
or stay closed like a fist

The Second Ghost
Cassandra Alexandra Soldo

What is seen cannot be unseen,
     But...
Can what has not yet been done simply never come to be?

When dreams are sensible,
They seep into reality.
Most go forgotten,
Returning in that moment,
Yet one has remained.

The vision haunts my mind,
Hiding in the depths,
And creeping to the surface.
It appears a warning of death,
Brings more than one ghost.

What is seen cannot be unseen,
     But...
Am I at fault if simply knowing makes it come to be?

Artemision
Kieran Rose Pilon

the forest and field are a hush of midnight stillness as arcane
cardstock slides against the boot-bruised stage, pulsing infinity
through our fingers, four new moonflowers blooming around a
deck of cards, and as the moon comes unclouded to wash the park
in glistening silver, brown fur shakes and antlers quake and from
the forest steps a deer, two, a mother and a fawn, and my heart
throbs out a new beat, owl eyes trained on cloven hooves and
white-spotted infancy, and the seven of us, flowers and deer and
the mother moon above, fall not into an abyss but a feather-soft
nook of a single breath.

The Empress (III)
Venus Astria

Twelve stars of gold adorn her diadem;
arils of pomegranate bejewel her dress.
With an earthly beauty like none other,
her presence serves as a symbol of divine opulence.

Upon her throne, she mirrors Venus;
her lustrous aura beams like a regal, white satin.
Ushering in a renaissance of creative power,
she births new life with a scepter in hand.

Fluttering
Allison Baldwin

In the space above the mountain, beyond our cocoon,
We see tiny robots, emoting. They move their limbs
In right angles. Without thought, they suck straws between
Their teeth, flutter gum wrappers,
spit in the leaves, their own dialects
too comfortable to confront.

We float above them, ripped clean. All color and stretch.
Once upon a time, we would land, on each shoulder,
But there exists no softness now. Our wings,
Slight touch, stampede, incinerate, burn.
We leave no scar. Once upon a time,
Marks meant there was still a chance,
Still hope. But there is no softness now.

We eavesdrop in the heat of fog.
Watch them count stones. They bang,
Scrap, split, create the illusion
Of surplus dirt. Hands rough and peeling
With their own tears.

They scream and colors shiver, clean,
Reach, sway, in the wind's comfort.

We could reach. We could sway.
But there is no softness there. Once upon a time,
The fog meant a clearing. Now, they are too busy
Curling in the ache of their own fear.

divination witch
Maverick L. Malone

tarot and tea leaves
runes
numerology
futures divined
from dowsing and scrying
clarity garnered from clairvoyance
prophecies and predictions
and ancient Greek wisdom
second sight distinctly designed
from peering behind veils
with all three eyes

Luna
Cece Rose Trezza

Did the moon tell you?
I wonder if she did.
She probably didn't mean to,
But she's an open book and terrible at
Poker.

If you look up at her dazzling shine,
Even for just a moment—
You'll understand the secrets of life,
And all the stories anyone has ever told her in confidence.
She doesn't even need to speak
And I'm just afraid she might have let my secrets slip.

So I really wonder if she told you about the nights I stayed up
late,
Staring at her pretty face, telling her
About yours.
She gets so excited for me.
She gets so excited with me.
She must have seen us laughing together on the that night
Because she likes you,
And she always likes whoever I tell her about,
But she especially likes you,

But maybe she didn't tell you.
She's gotten better at keeping secrets,
Hiding her expressive smile and shine behind
A grey fog,
But still she's a loud mouth,
Loves to talk about all things pretty,
Says I'm the prettiest.

She was dark,
and new,
the cold December night I had that breakthrough.
When I realized you were who I wanted,
Who I needed,
And even though I couldn't see her,
I could feel her elation from a thousand miles away,
Her lunar essence swaying in the breeze.

She's a great listener,
A friend,
Therapist,
Offering cosmically crafted advice and ethereal explanations
Through signs
Through songs,
Through birds,
Through feelings,
Synchronicities.

I think her little star sisters are in on it too,
sending their own rays of hope and knowledge,
But I like it
Because it makes it feel like the whole universe is rooting for us.

And she was full the night I couldn't stop crying.
God I really hope she didn't tell you—
That's embarrassing.
I know she hurt the same way I did that night
After you took those pills,
Watching as I clutched the corduroy couch cushion until my nails
tore the fabric,
Praying that you were okay,
Praying that she would help you,
Praying you were protected.
Me and her were one that night

She laughs sometimes,
And I really never know why.
Does she think I'm funny?
Or does she know something I don't;
That maybe you whisper those same things about me to her too?

But she's still a just the moon and it's hard to believe sometimes
that something is there,
That our connection exists,
so far and silent at times,
But I know it does.
I can tell the way she shines.
It's just like me and you.

You're just like her
and I think that's why I like you.

XXI The World and II The Mystery
Flor Ana

calming the chaos that crosses the clouds,
the shadow of a deer lies still in the ground.
it brings with it gentleness, innocence,
even as it moves.
then, you spot three intuitive eyes instead of two,
and you ask yourself if
everything you see is really what it means.

the deer dashes across the forest floor
and you know this leg of your journey is no more.
you have graduated
to the nine teacups,
the ones with the flowers painted on the cusps
of showing you a whole new journey,
one where success is already awaiting you.

Untitled
Ruth Camillia

What role does divination have among the revolution?
What purpose does it serve to speak of dreams, numbers,
afterlife, and all the in between?
Sometimes the waking life feels so confined.
Sometimes the constructs and systems defined
amount to more angst and resistance.
The liminal space of the astral planes
is where hope is stored.
We weave in and out of these thoughts and ideas
for comfort, peace, and the possibility of new beginnings.
Fairies, angels, and deceased loved ones can meet with us here.
In the in-between, no one is ever alone.
The sounds of nature, rattles, and drums
guide us to where we belong.
In meditation, we can imagine ourselves back in the womb.
We can visualize the glow of reds and golden hues,
the whooshing sounds of fluids cradling us like a buoy bobbing
in the ocean's waves.
Distant humming, talking, or singing reminds us of
the promise of a welcome committee. When you're ready,
you'll always find your family.
We curl up tight in the shape of shrimps or crescent moons
resting quietly there.
We do this in remembrance.
We make ourselves small to feel safe.
We make these connections and find reflections in all the
shapes and symbols.
A resistance toward parenthood or our own parents
can be neutralized by coming back to our prenatal selves.
Who was I before the blending of semen and cells?
What was it that my parents hoped for, dreamt about, and feared?
I come back to this sack of light, love, and gentle vibration.

For months before labor my limbs grew and my face
formed there.
In the womb, our souls are reborn.

The Prayer of the Tarot
M. Watkins

Let me have the heart of the *Fool*,

that I may meet each new situation

with innocence and wonder.

******

Let me have the eye of the *Emperor*,

that I may see both near and far

for the things I am truly responsible for.

******

Let me have the enthusiasm of the

Empress, creativity to fill the world with

wonderous things.

******

Let me have the knowing of the *Priestess*,

to have the words and intonations to shape

from energy that which is needed and

wanted at the right time.

******

Let me hold the power of *Balance*, to

keep my feet untroubled as I walk around

this world.

******

Let me have the knowing and faith to

share my experience in this space with

those who need it as the *Hierophant*.

******

Let me have the light of the *Star*, that I

may see where I am going in that high

distant place.

******

Let me have the pull of the *Moon*, that I

may guide the lost and weary, the lonely

and confused.

******

Let me shine like the *Sun*, to help those

foundlings grow, ripen, mature into their

true-selves.

******

Let me have the soul of the *Hermit*, to

know when to journey and when to retreat

into myself, that I may repair and nurture

the light within.

Goddess of Divine Energy
Alicia Ayala (Blue Mystic)

You say
my all is too much
too overwhelming

But I'm the one
who is sorry
for expecting
a human to understand
the depth and beauty
of divine emotion

XV - *The Devil*
Emily Long

I'm writing this poem between stoplights scrawled on my wrist
as I drive home from therapy, where I once again spent an hour
trying to explain my depression in a way that doesn't
make either of us the villain. I'm trying

to befriend her sweeter, hold her hand, reckon
with her fist against my jaw, the same fingers
outstretched a moment later to wipe dead leaves
falling from my cheeks.

The top card on my tarot deck today is the Devil,
Baphomet and his goat skull ready for the sacrifice,
our bent knees bleeding. The shackles that bind us
so clearly of our own making, so easily slipped loose.

If you loved me, you might say my depression is the devil
on my shoulder, but I'm not sure I believe in heaven
or hell anymore, beyond the bluebird blaze of binaries
going up in flames. We carry constellations and wildfires

in our marrow and the tarot tells me to release
everything I've been clinging to so tight,
white knuckles aching and that bottomless blue
tapping my shoulder, tempting me to loosen my grip.

I pull out my pen after hiking up 13,000 feet
to write another ending but for once,
while I balance on the knife edge,
I don't want to think about dying.

At the red light heading home, I set down questions of Purpose
with that capital P. Even though I know we all become periods

some day, I say today I will be a comma, a hyphen,
a dash of curiosity and more to come

as the light turns
green.

three card tarot spread
Tova Greene

my was deserves a funeral shroud.
it's a tad short notice (jews don't
get sundays off) so instead of thread
i'm sewing with frizzy brown hair &
lanyard. the pattern accounts for three
blocks.it took me all night to collect
fabric; what i saw in my hands as
the sun rose were:

4 trash bags of leaves, 6 jars of applesauce, the license plate of
my mom's buick, the plastic wrapping of the first weed i ever saw
in the back of a car, shards of a disco ball, xylophone blocks,
leather of a baseball that stung my hand when my dad threw it too
hard, gum wrappers kicked under desks, receipts of arizona iced
teas & mike & ikes, mismatched flip flops, dust from an attic filled
with broken drum sets, fur discarded by felix the outdoor cat, &
long-forgotten secret codes.

my now breathes through one nostril &
out the other, spots my will be blurred
behind subway cars, gently kisses my
was' forehead, & throws 1000 yellow
daisies, gasoline & a match on her.
with golden tears & a misty rainfall
the trees join their whispered farewell
davening.

Hermit
Allison Baldwin

Such loneliness is harrowing,
such light translucent. Introspection
invited into the narrow hall,
between the kitchen—covered in coffee cups
and crumbs, a half-washed knife—
(what cream cheese delights in obtusely cut
bagels? we are not so perfect.) The music plays
beyond the light, lips syncing, puckering beyond
each coiled measure. Silence is its own melody,
a ringing ear. Hands held out, closed petals.
The hum-drum heartbeat of aliveness,
tightly contained in other words:

Rage. Heartbreak
Bound(aries) and yet,
there is always a tunnel
of lanterns. The end of cyclical cylinders.

There is a whale in the next room
(the other half)
blowing air. Like Collins, I long
to climb on its back, crawl into its mouth
see the peak of my obsession. Perspective
is two parallel lines, multiplied. With time,
(such a long way off) everything

Kaleidoscopes and bends.
Intricacies become obvious
normality. Everything is (re)new(ed)

and Justice has prevailed.

The Lovers
Angelica Medlin

It was the five of swords
The night I asked the universe
To give me a sign
But the emptiness of the bed next to me
Should have spoken volumes
Long before I drew

I waited on the next draw
And when his words stung my chest
When his hands met my flesh
I drew
Knowing long before
That I'd pull the tower

The next draw was longer
My deck sitting silent atop my dusty altar
But his lips were sweet
His hands were warm
And when the magic returned to my veins
I drew again

THE POETS

A. K. A. is a Miami-based poet who finds inspiration in nature. Her flourishing curiosity in the metaphysical world began at a young age when she discovered and indebted herself to the Wiccan religion. The deep connection she feels toward the divine universe has driven her to dedicate her life to esoteric teachings, such as tarot card reading, energy healing, and spiritual guidance. A.K.A. uses her relationship with nature to create thought-provoking poems that invoke an emotional link between the natural and spiritual worlds.
Instagram: @dappy_doe

Flor Ana is a Cuban-American writer, artist and poet born in Bauta, Cuba and raised in Miami, Florida. She debuted as an author with her self-published poetry collection, *Perspective (and other poems)*, which went on to become a bestseller at Barnes & Noble locations around South Florida. Since her debut, Flor has released two more poetry collections: *The Language of Fungi & Flowers* and *Nourish Your Temple: Self-Love & Care Poetry*. Flor is the editor-in-chief of Indie Earth Publishing and is continuing to write her own books and help other writers. // *Instagram: @littleearthflower*

Venus Astria is a lover of mythology, astronomy, spirituality, and philosophy. After an insightful astrology reading, she aligned her first post on Instagram with the 2022 New Moon in Aries and immediately fell in love with the supportive poetry community. Venus most enjoys the melodic nature of poetry and believes it to be a powerful mode for healing and discovering personal philosophies. Her poems touch on Greek mythology, cosmology, and the human experience. She currently resides in Denver, Colorado. // *Instagram: @venusastria*

Alicia Ayala (aka Blue Mystic) is a singer, songwriter, poet, and multidimensional artist from Miami, Florida. Her music and poetry showcase a natural ability to connect with universal flow to channel emotion, soul experiences, and spiritual wisdom. Transmuting darkness into light and expanding consciousness is the driving force behind her craft. She aims to comfort and inspire others on their healing journey as they collectively strive for self-mastery. With her otherworldly, cosmic essence and thought-provoking quotes, she dives deep into the streams of consciousness of her audience. The pieces featured in *The Spell Jar: Poetry for the Modern Witch* are channeled messages. // *Instagram: @_bluemystic*

Allison Baldwin is a poet and disability advocate based in New Jersey. She is currently pursuing her MFA in Poetry and Poetic Medicine through Dominican University of California's low-residency creative writing program. Her literary interests include ekphrasis, erasure poetry, prose poetry, one-hundred-word stories, novels-in-verse, and critical essays, with several pieces published in print and online, including Dominican's Tuxedo Arts Journal. Additionally, Allison has seven years of experience reading tarot and loves using poetry to translate card energy. // *Instagram: @the_awakened_poet*

Victoria Lynn Beckett is the author of *Learning to Swim While Drowning*, a collection of poetry and essays. Victoria hopes you, the reader, are in love—that reality-bending state of pure elation that makes all things possible and bearable. From girlhood to adulthood, she has been enamored with tales of great big worlds conquered by brave, passionate heroines. Her writing focuses on the power of romance, the inner emotional universe, journeys of growth, and above all, love.
Instagram: @violetvicxenvignettes

Ruth Camillia is a bilingual, bicultural, queer, and enby healing arts practitioner and literary artist. They reside on Tongva and Acjachemen land in their hometown of Santa Ana, California. With maternal Indigeneous roots from Los Altos de Jalisco, México, they integrate ancestral practices into their daily life and work. Ruth has a Bachelors in Spanish Language and Literature from UC Berkeley and currently works part-time as a youth mentor and book advisor at their local book-store and literary arts space, LibroMobile.
Instagram: @ruth_camillia

Madeleine S. Cargile studies neuroscience at Auburn University as a member of its honors college and has had multiple works of short fiction and poetry published in small-pub an-thologies and literary magazines. Among reading and writing, she enjoys art, embroidery, and heavy metal music.
Instagram: @madeleinescargilewrites

Victoria Clara is a writer who was born in Las Piedras, Uru-guay, raised in Miami, Florida, and now resides in the con-crete jungle of New York City. A lover of painting and music, Victoria takes inspirations for her writing from a cool breeze and fellow artists. *The Spell Jar: Poetry for the Modern Witch* is her literary debut. // *Instagram: @notaraptillian*

Christian Colado is a poet who thrives off strange and surreal ideas, and is constantly looking for new ways to incorporate his experiences into his work. A good laugh can always be found in his presence. You can find him dreaming about the swampy green Everglades, or the sandy beaches in Florida.
Instagram: @writingindreams

*Andy Daniel Diaz (*aka addingpassion) was born and raised in Miami, Florida. Powered by his heart and centered by his breath, Andy's goal is to add passion everywhere he goes,

whether at work as an accountant or on stage as a poet and sto-
ryteller. He shares his poetry on Instagram and believes there
is always an opportunity to add passion to your life and the
lives of others if you slow your mind and open your heart.
Instagram: @addingpassion

Athena Edwards was born and raised in a small coastal town
in North Carolina, but she has never let her location stop her
from learning about the world. After graduating with a Mas-
ter's in Composition, Rhetoric, and Digital Media, she works
hard as an editor and writer to help provide a voice to under-
represented and hidden voices and for the people who need to
hear them. Some of her past poems can be read in the Digres-
sions Literary and Art Journal (Volumes 17-19).
Instagram: @aquawave23

Jacquelynne Faith is a lifelong writer, having written her first
book, *Mi Trip 2 New Yorc,* before she could even spell. Now,
she spells in many ways with a background in professional
copywriting and editing, a degree in Human Communication
from UCF, and a career as an oracle and priestess (for real!).
You can also find her stepping into her magic in the form of
witches, sirens, and mermaids as a professional model and
credited actress. // *Instagram: @jacquelynnefaith*

Rachel Finkle is a writer whose favorite fruits are grapes.
They write a lot, but not as much as they feel they should.
Rachel is studying healthcare and hopes their poetry can work
with medicine to heal others like it has for them. Their debut
collection, *Raspberry Fingers,* will be out January 31, 2023
Instagram: @rachel.e.f

Courtney Force is a mystic poet and soul guide. Through her
coaching business, Forcefield, Courtney supports people in
connecting with their soul and improving their mental, emotio-

nal, spiritual, and physical health. She is a certified Master Usui Reiki Healer, Soul Memory Discovery Facilitator, and Breathwork Facilitator, and holds a Bachelor's Degree in Communication from San Diego State University. Her debut collection of poetry, *Soul Dancer*, was published in August 2022. When she is not traveling the world with her partner, Courtney can be found nurturing her roots at one of her homes in England or California. // *Instagram: @courtneyforcefield*

Tova Greene is a non-binary, queer, Jewish poet who recently graduated with a Bachelor in Liberal Arts from Sarah Lawrence College in Yonkers, New York. Their debut collection, *lilac on the damned's breath*, was published in June of 2022. They are also currently working on their second book of poetry, *ohso*. Their work has been featured in Eunoia Review, Midway Journal, Love & Squalor, Clickbait, Soul Talk Magazine, & Primavera Zine. They currently live in Manhattan with their partner and cat. // *Instagram: @tovagreene*

Johanna Hatch is a poet writing at the intersections of kinship, nature, and magic. A lifelong writer, Johanna's first published poem appeared in the Millerton News of Millerton, New York at age 7. As an adult, her essays have appeared in anthologies and national magazines. Johanna is trained as a nurse and midwife, and the cycles of life inspire her spirituality and writing. A native of Cape Cod, Massachusetts, she currently lives in Wisconsin with her husband and two children. *Instagram: @johannajanet*

Trudy Hodnefield is a queer writer and maker of Japanese descent from Oʻahu, Hawaii. She received a BA in English Literature and Creative Writing from Seattle University and is pursuing an MA in Fashion Studies at Parsons School of Design. Her work has been published in the Hawaii Review and BIAS Journal of Dress Practice, with forthcoming poems to be included in SOFT QTRLY. Her work focuses on memory, identity, home, and the relationship each has with the body. *Instagram: @dickache*

Amelie Honeysuckle is a student at the University of Colorado Boulder who loves spending her time meandering through her local trails on bike and foot. Amelie is a lover of words and believes that one of the most beautiful ways to colorfully create is through the art of words. Amelie loves finding unconventional beauty in her environment, thrives through writing love poetry for her people, and is a believer that "you make your own happiness." // *Instagram: @wordsbyamelie*

Kendall Hope is a Colorado native, who thrives off of sunshine and has been a creative since the time she was small. She loves exploring the outdoors and being a part of nature—with the self-recognition that she is nature—which translates to her poetry. Always working toward the next creative step, Kendall finds satisfaction in the little things, which help her stay present. Her debut poetry collection, *Pockets of Lavender*, was published August 2022.
Instagram: @kendallhopepoetry

Sofia Iriarte is a Barcelona-born poet and author who migrated to the Florida at the age of 16 and is studying Communications at Florida International University. Sofia made her literary debut at the age of 12 with her poem "El Jardí De La Vida," which was published in a magazine in Barcelona. Sofia thrives off cryptic wording and metaphors to express herself in her poetry and never fully knows what's on her mind. *Bravery, Heart & Red Shoes* is Sofia's first full collection of poetry detailing her coming of age journey from Spain to the US and her feelings throughout. It will be out November 18, 2022.
Instagram: @siriartte

Laura Beth Johnson is an award-winning poet and songwriter based in Upstate New York. She was awarded the Lucy Monro Brooker Poetry Prize in 2017 and a Songwriting Fellowship by Image Magazine in 2019. Her poetry has been published in journals and collections with Post Mortem Press, Lady Blue Publishing, Etchings Press, The Lanthorn and now Indie Earth Publishing. You can find her music on all streaming platforms under the moniker "Sorrow Estate."
Instagram: @laurabethwrites

Hayden Kasal-Barsky is a sophomore attending the University of Hawaii at Manoa. She's currently studying Elementary Education and Special Education. Hayden dreams of becoming Poet Laureate one day, as well as an international poet. She believes beauty is in everything especially words and nature. *The Spell Jar: Poetry for the Modern Witch* is Hayden's debut.
Instagram: @hayden.officiall

Kimberly Kling enjoys writing poetry from her home in the high desert of Southern Arizona where she also explores homesteading with her family, adventuring around the rivers and mountains, and creating herbal magic with the plants she grows and tends in her Joyful Roots Ranch gardens. The Earth is her informant to life's lessons, and it is through the alchemy of observing the world around her and studying herself that her poems take life. // *Instagram: @joyfulroots*

Emily Long is a queer writer living in Denver, Colorado. A winner of the 2021 True Colors poetry prize with Vocal Media & Moleskine, Emily has also been published in Anti-Heroin Chic, Quail Bell Magazine, & Passengers Journal, among others. When Emily is not writing, you'll find them paddleboarding, hiking, and climbing in the Rocky Mountains with their partner and rescue pup. // *Instagram: @emdashemi*

Maverick L. Malone is an East Tennessee writer, poet, and self-proclaimed "unearther of life." She believes in the magic of language as a powerful tool for alchemy, healing, and inner truth. Though Maverick has always considered herself a writer, it wasn't until 2020 when her gifts were reignited, and she dove headfirst into making her dreams a reality. Maverick's debut poetry collection, *Pressed Petals*, is slated to release in late 2022. // *Instagram: @mavmalone*

Amalia Maria is a poet and creative nonfiction writer from Miami, Florida and is currently pursuing her B.A in Creative Writing from the University of Central Florida. Amalia's writing ranges from intimate poetry to nonfiction essays, written creatively using techniques from writing workshops. *Instagram: @amaliamariaps*

Angelica Medlin is an English graduate student at California State University of Fullerton (CSUF) in sunny Southern California where she lives with her partner and sassy dog. She has worked in academia for nearly a decade as a writing and English tutor and educator, and has worked for CSUF's DASH literary journal for two years. Currently, she is completing her first novel as she finishes up the last year of her Master's degree program. // *Instagram: @thebrujapoeta*

Chelsea Miner is a lifelong poet and storyteller whose work is inspired by the liminal spaces within the human experience. Her interest in secular witchcraft began in childhood, and the subject now informs much of her creative work, including her poetry. She studied English Literature and Journalism at Peru State College, where she was involved in Sigma Tau Delta: an International English Honor Society. Chelsea now lives in Omaha, Nebraska with her son, Oliver, and husband, Andrew. *Instagram: @by_c.a.miner*

Jacob R. Moses (aka Jack M. Freedman) is a poet and spoken word artist from Staten Island, New York. Publications featuring his work span the globe. He is the author of the full-length poetry book, *Grimoire*, and is currently a graduate student at Southern New Hampshire University, pursuing a Masters in English Literature and Creative Writing. Each poem in this anthology was an assignment.
Instagram: @jacobreubenmoses

Mia Mourn is a Los Angeles-based writer, photographer, and small business owner, selling various handcrafted bookish gifts and accessories. Mia has had many hobbies and artistic passions, but poetry has always held a special place in her heart. She considers poetry to be her first love, and although the trials and tribulations of adulthood caused her to pull away from her writing, Mia has finally found her way back to poetry and is making her poetic debut in *The Spell Jar: Poetry for the Modern Witch*. // *Instagram: @broodingromantic*

Jordan Nishkian is an Armenian-Portuguese writer based in California. Her prose and poetry explore themes of duality and have been featured in national and international publications. She is the editor-in-chief of Mythos literary magazine and author of *Kindred*, a novella. // *Instagram: @wordsbyjordan*

Clair O'Connor is a California native currently living in a coastal town. She enjoys a variety of art mediums and started exploring poetry at the beginning of the pandemic as a means to help her mental health. Since then, she has written over 200 pieces and will have her publishing debut in *The Spell Jar: Poetry for the Modern Witch*. Clair draws inspiration from the natural world and inner processing.
Instagram: @clairoconnorr

Alexa Park is a licensed, experienced literature and creative writing teacher who holds two Masters degrees. She has taught a range of students, from kindergarten to college, in both public and progressive private school environments. Now a full-time mama, Lex no longer teaches full-time. She still writes everyday, and hosts writing workshops. Lex finds inspiration in nature, and discovers her creative voice at the intersection of the simple and the profound.

Kieran Rose Pilon is a CreWri-certified theatre major from Minnesota. He's been writing for as long as he can remember, and has been published in such journals as Substantially (Un)limited, Moss Puppy, and Filter Coffee, along with the anthology, *Horror Without Borders*. His current projects are a folk horror-comedy screenplay, a gothic horror zombie novel, and a poetry chapbook titled *Home for Harrowed Men*. Kieran's works often revolve around heartbreak and other traumas.
Twitter: @krpilon

John Queor is a queer poet, scribbling most of his work while cloaked in the early morning darkness. John resides in central New York, but one day hopes to live in Maine, in a small cottage by the sea. John is in the process of releasing his debut poetry collection, *Burnt Lavender*, and is working on another book to be published in the near future.
Instagram: @johnnyqu33r

Lianne Quintero is a 26-year-old queer woman, who currently resides in Miami, Florida and is a full-time yoga instructor. Lianne is a multifaceted woman who also loves to write. Her pieces consist of erotic poetry and the dynamics of divine masculine and feminine energies. She's currently working on a Patreon platform and *The Spell Jar: Poetry for the Modern Witch* is her publishing debut. // *Instagram: @_lillsss*

Marissa Renee is a Northern California native, and an artist of many forms. She particularly enjoys painting, photography, and poetry. Aside from her creative interests, Marissa is a tarot reader and Reiki practitioner, who specializes in Usui and Reiki Seichem. Marissa takes inspiration from the subtle energies she perceives in the world and from the dreams and clairvoyant visions which flow through her. *The Spell Jar: Poetry For the Modern Witch* is her debut as a poet.
Instagram: @dream_wxtch

Elyse Rintelman (aka voidbird) is a trans woman who works as a writer and video editor in Albany, New York. In her free time, Elyse talks to her cats and acoustic guitar, in the hope that they will bring her good luck. *The Spell Jar: Poetry for the Modern Witch* is her publishing debut.
Instagram: @mufflepopdontstop

Tess Rio is a writer and artist from Central California, who, after minoring in English at a state college and receiving a certificate in Design Communication Arts from UCLA Extension, decided to combine her education to create art and poetry. Not long after the fact, Tess discovered her path in witchcraft. Her hope is to use words to enchant the world, one poem at a time.
Instagram: @themagickofarte

Darya Rose is a queer Bay Area native who received their Bachelors degree in Sociology. They have been writing poetry since they were 12 and wrote for the Odyssey while in college. They spend their free time exploring the mind and nature, utilizing tarot in their creative endeavors, and communing with spirits. *The Spell Jar: Poetry for the Modern Witch* is Darya's literary debut. // *Instagram: @daryarostami*

Kira Rosemarie is a writer and artist from Kentucky, currently living in South Florida. She writes short fiction and poetry, and

has had works published in Sad Girls Club Literary Blog, The Dillydoun Review, and Cathexis Northwest Press.
Instagram: @busy_witch

Javon Rustin started performing and competing in poetry slams while at North Carolina Agricultural and Technical State University where he received his Bachelor of Science in Computer Science. He grew up in Durham, North Carolina, and currently resides in Maryland. His poetry has been published in six anthologies, along with online publications such as I Am Hip Hop Magazine (London). His spoken word can be heard on Button Poetry and Write About Now Youtube channels. When not performing, Javon spends time with loved ones, bikes, and books. // *Instagram: @javonrustin*

Cassandra Alexandra Soldo was born and raised in New Jersey and is a current student at Agnes Scott College in Decatur, Georgia, where she is pursuing degrees in Creative Writing and Psychology. Ever since she was little, Cassandra has experienced visions of the future through her dreams, which is the inspiration for her featured poem, "The Second Ghost." *The Spell Jar: Poetry for the Modern Witch* is Cassandra's poetic debut. // *Instagram: @cassandra_soldo*

Veronica Szymankiewicz is a published poet from Miami, Florida, whose poetry is directly inspired by her own personal experiences, thoughts, and feelings. A lifelong writer and lover of words, she considers poetry a cathartic outlet. Veronica writes as a way to heal herself, with the hopes that her words will resonate with others, healing them along the way. Her poems have been published in RDW and The Lit Tribune.
Instagram: @verorisingpoetry

Cece Rose Trezza is a happy-go-lucky fourth-year screenwriting student at Loyola Marymount University's School of Film and Television. A jack of all trades, Cece loves to write, sing, draw, act, freestyle, dance, and perform standup. Their art focuses on battling mental illness, working through trauma, and finding oneself and community through the use of spirituality. Their debut musical, "Spiritual Awakening," performed at the 2022 New Works Festival, encapsulates these same themes as their poem, "Luna." // *Instagram: @cece_hehe_*

Lindsay Valentin is a writer and creative artist residing in Los Angeles, California. She has written poetry, fiction and nonfiction on travel, culture, lightwork, and lesbian life, in print and online, for GO NYC Magazine, BUST Magazine, Defy Magazine, Pink Pangea, and Querencia press. She works deeply with herbs and reiki, and is a part of the West Coast mystic and sound healing community. // *Instagram: @lvalentin77*

Heidi Valkenburg is a queer, multi-disciplined artist from Naarm, Australia, who resides in Lenapehoking / Brooklyn, New York. Heidi works predominantly within performance, visual art and written word. Their work is often introspective, dreamy, amusing, and forever exploring the intricacies of the human condition whilst deeply inspired by the natural world. Heidi is currently working on their first collection of poetry, *fae blood*, due for release in late 2022.
Instagram: @heidivalkenburg

Annie Vazquez is a poet, writer, and former freelance journalist featured in the Miami Herald, Refinery29, NBC6, and Vogue. Her blog, The Fashion Poet, is Miami's #1 lifestyle blog and her wellness brand, Annie the Alchemist, has been featured on People Magazine, Man Repellar, and Time Out Magazine. Annie has published ebooks on self-love and wellness, and has released an affirmation deck titled *Affirmations for Abundance*. Her debut poetry collection will be released in 2023. *Instagram: @anniewriteswords / @anniethealchemist*

M. Watkins is a spiritual eclectic writer, artist and poet who resides in the state of Georgia, though she really believes we all are natives of somewhere else. Her poem, "The Prayer of the Tarot" is a contemplation of how we can use these well-known images and ideas to lead us in new directions. She is currently working on an Oracle deck and book, in which both the images and messages are a collaboration between herself and guides. // *Instagram: @thebtfgazette*

INDIE EARTH
PUBLISHING

About The Publisher

Indie Earth Publishing is an author-first, independent publishing company based in Miami, FL, dedicated to giving artists and writers the creative freedom they deserve in publishing their poetry, fiction, and short stories. We provide our authors a plethora of services that are meant to make them feel like they are finally releasing the book of their dreams, including professional editing, design, formatting, organization, advanced reader teams, and so much more. With Indie Earth Publishing, you're more than just another author, you're part of the Indie Earth creative family, making a difference in the world, one book at a time.

www.indieearthbooks.com

For inquiries, please email:
indieearthpublishinghouse@gmail.com

Instagram: @indieearthbooks